TIMELY
INTERVENTION

MOHAMED SANUSIE TRAORE

ACKNOWLEDGEMENTS

My special thanks to my entire family for their love and support and my immense gratitude to my communities in the USA, Guinea, and Sierra Leone for their amazing support. My fellow immigrant community here in the USA and around the world you showed me I am not alone in our efforts to build a brighter future for ourselves and our fellow humanity. I thank you a lot. I hope my humble stories will inspire millions of people around the world. Once again, my immense gratitude to everyone.

TABLE OF CONTENTS

A TIMELY INTERVENTION

In a world consumed by screens and disarray,
Where empathy seems to fade and dismay,
Amidst the chaos, a hero arose,
A modern-day savior, in the shadows he chose.

An Uber driver, his cape unseen,
With a heart of gold, his purpose keen,
Through bustling streets, he embarked each
 day, A guardian angel in a mundane array.

Destiny's whispers guided his way,
To those in need, he'd swiftly sway,
A beacon of hope, a timely light,
A guardian angel veiled in the night.
In a time when tragedy strikes with force,
When compassion takes a backseat, remorse,
He defied the norm, stood tall and brave,

To lend a helping hand, a soul to save.

In a world entranced by digital tales,
 Where virtual reality often prevails,
People stood frozen, lost in their screens,
Captivated spectators of unfolding scenes.

But he, the hero of our tale,
Saw beyond the pixels, through the veil,
When others filmed, detached and remote,
He stepped forward, offering hope.

One fateful eve, a call for aid,
A family in peril, their lives betrayed,
A crash of metal, a soul's descent,
Their cries were unheard, their pleas unmeant.

With lightning speed, he raced to the scene,
 No time to spare, their fate obscene,
In a flurry of bravery, he pulled them free,
A mother and daughter, his resolute decree.

Minutes elapsed, an explosion ensued,
Flames danced wildly, the car imbued,
 But safe they stood, under his watchful eye,
Rescued from danger, their souls set to fly.

Yet recognition eluded his humble frame,
CBS local press hailed his heroic name,

No accolades adorned his Uber profile,

But in the hearts he touched, his deeds would compile.

For it's not in the spotlight that heroes thrive,

But in the selfless acts that keep hope alive,

In a world enamored with fame and pretense,

He chose compassion, his only defense.

He stood as a symbol, a shining light,

In the face of apathy, shining bright,

This a reminder to all, in times of despair,

To offer a helping hand, to show we care.

May his story inspire, ignite the flame,

To help those in need, to never be tame,

For in the darkest of times, in moments most dire,

Timely intervention can rekindle the fire.

So let us rise above, the allure of the screen,

And in the footsteps of heroes, let us convene,

To extend a helping hand, with love and affection,

For in each timely intervention, lies true perfection.

Let's break the cycle of indifference's grip,

Embrace our humanity, let compassion equip us,

For when tragedy strikes and hearts break asunder,

It's not the cameras we need, but a touch of wonder.

So put down your phones, extend a hand,
Unite as one, let empathy expand,
For in the tapestry of life, when tragedy's near,
It's the heroes among us who erase the fear.

In a world longing for connection and care,
Be the one who answers when others just stare,
A timely intervention, a beacon of hope,
A testament to humanity, a boundless scope.

And so, we honor the hero's noble quest,
This a reminder to us all, at our very best,
In the face of tragedy, when darkness looms,
It's compassion that triumphs and truly consumes.

For in a world consumed by screens and despair,
Let's be the timely intervention, the souls who dare,
To lift each other, to bridge the divide,
In acts of kindness, let love reside.

So let us rise above, the allure of the screen,
And in the footsteps of heroes, let us convene,
To extend a helping hand, with love and affection,
For in each timely intervention, lies true perfection.

CHAPTER 1

EMPATHY , COMPASSION, AND CHARITY

Empathy*: the ability to understand and share the feelings, experiences, and perspectives of others. It involves putting oneself in someone else's shoes and truly comprehending their emotions and thoughts, often leading to a sense of compassion and the desire to alleviate their suffering. Empathy allows individuals to connect with others on a deeper level, fostering understanding, kindness, and support in interpersonal relationships and society as a whole.*

I am someone who lives my life by helping people in need every day. This value was instilled in me from a young age while growing up in Africa. I strongly believe that parents and schools should teach children the importance of caring for one another. I think as people, we should prioritize human connection over material things. It saddens me to see how often people reach for their phones to record an incident instead of offering a helping hand. While technology is important, we seem to have lost the ability to truly connect with one another.

I believe in helping others because it's something I learned early on in my life. In today's world, it's disheartening to see empathy dwindling among people. Instead of rushing to help someone in need, many people immediately grab their phones to record the situation. It's as if we've lost the ability to connect with others on a basic human level. We've become more focused on capturing dramatic moments and seeking online validation than genuinely caring for others.

Technology, especially smartphones, has become an integral part of our lives. Social media platforms and the need for online recognition have intensified our desire to capture and share everything. We're drawn to the spectacle and the attention it brings, even at the expense of real human connection. Screens dominate our attention, causing us to overlook the faces and stories of those who require our help. We've become passive observers, rather than active participants in the lives of others.

In this sea of digital distractions, there are still individuals who choose empathy over virtual documentation. They are the unsung heroes, the compassionate souls who risk their own safety to help those in distress. Their stories inspire us, reminding us that we all have the capacity for empathy within us. They show us that even small acts of kindness can make a difference.

Reconnecting with empathy requires a conscious effort to break free from the influence of technology. We need to shift our priorities and prioritize genuine human connection. It means recognizing the allure of capturing everything and actively choosing empathy instead. Rather than reaching for our phones, we should extend a helping hand and be present in the moment. We should value face-to-face interactions and foster meaningful relationships.

Cultivating empathy in the digital age requires a comprehensive approach. We should be mindful of our screen time, setting limits and boundaries. By reducing our smartphone usage and being fully present, we become more aware of the needs of others and can cultivate empathy. We should also use technology responsibly, using it as a tool for connection rather than a barrier. Instead of using our devices for self-promotion, we should engage with others, listen to their stories, and understand their struggles.

Education also plays a crucial role in nurturing empathy. It's important to teach children about empathy, kindness, and compassion from a young age. By creating a culture that values empathy, we can empower young minds to navigate the digital world with compassion. Community involvement is equally important. Empathy thrives when we actively engage with those around us and address the needs of our communities. Through volunteering, participating in community service, and advocating for social justice, we can bridge the empathy gap and build a society that values compassion and understanding.

In rekindling empathy, we must remember that it's a choice we make every day, regardless of the technological landscape. We have the power to break free from the distractions and truly care for others. By stepping away from the allure of capturing everything and embracing genuine human connection, we can bridge the gaps created by digital distractions. Together, we can create a world where acts of kindness and understanding prevail.

In conclusion, the decline of empathy in our society is concerning. However, there are still individuals who embody empathy in its truest form. They remind us of the transformative power of compassion and inspire us to be agents of positive change. By reclaiming empathy, nurturing genuine human connections, and breaking free from digital distractions.

Compassion: A deep feeling of sympathy, care, and concern for the suffering, hardships, or misfortunes of others. It involves recognizing and acknowledging the pain or struggles someone is experiencing and having a genuine desire to alleviate their suffering or offer support. Compassion goes beyond empathy, as it not only involves understanding another person's emotions but also actively taking action to help, comfort, or provide assistance in any way possible. It is characterized by kindness, selflessness, and a willingness to show empathy through acts of compassion and understanding.

When was the last time you showed someone compassion? Have you ever taken a moment to truly understand and empathize with their struggles, and offer them comfort in your own unique way? Showing compassion doesn't cost anything; it's a simple act of kindness that can make a world of difference to someone in need. Just imagine if you were in their shoes – wouldn't you appreciate someone stepping up and showing you compassion?

I believe in treating others the way I want to be treated. Recently, I experienced the loss of my mother, and during that difficult time, I was fortunate to have many people come forward and offer their help in any way they could. It was heartening to see that my mother's compassionate nature had touched so many lives. It made me proud of the upbringing I had, witnessing my parents' care and concern for others. As a result, I strive to show compassion every day of my life.

What also filled me with pride was seeing people who didn't even know my mother personally showing up to support me and extend their compassion. They selflessly stood by my side, offering their assistance without hesitation. It reminded me that when you treat people with kindness, they often reciprocate in the same way. Although I don't show compassion with the expectation of receiving it in return, it feels fulfilling to receive love and respect from others. It reinforces my belief that being a compassionate person is a reflection of the values instilled in me since childhood.

I was raised to consider the struggles and emotions of others. It is a core part of who I am as a person. While it is heartwarming to receive compassion, my motivation to show compassion stems from the desire to be the best version of myself and to help others whenever they are in need.

So, I ask you sincerely: When was the last time you showed someone compassion? I challenge you, as you read this book, to take a moment and truly observe the people around you. See what they may be going through and find ways to offer your support. Let go of judgment and embrace compassion instead. Sometimes, a simple hug or a few words of wisdom can make all the difference in someone's life. Put yourself in their shoes and show them the understanding and care they deserve. By fostering more compassion, we can collectively create a better world for all.

Charity: *the act of voluntarily giving assistance, support, or resources to those in need or to organizations and causes that aim to improve the well-being of others. It is a selfless act of kindness and generosity, typically motivated by compassion and a desire to make a positive impact in the lives of individuals or communities facing challenges.*

Charity can take various forms, including providing financial aid, donating goods or services, offering time and skills through volunteer work, or advocating for social change. It is often associated with addressing issues such as poverty, hunger, homelessness, education, healthcare, and environmental sustainability. The purpose of charity is to alleviate suffering, promote human welfare, and contribute to the betterment of society as a whole.

At its core, charity is driven by empathy and a deep concern for the well-being of others. It embodies the belief that every person deserves dignity, compassion, and the opportunity to thrive. Through acts of charity, individuals and organizations can help bridge gaps, uplift those in need, and create a more equitable and compassionate world.

Charity comes in many forms, ranging from the simplest acts of kindness to more organized efforts to support individuals or causes. For me, giving back is an integral part of my life, and I strive to make a difference whenever I can. I am deeply grateful for the people who stepped up to help me when I first arrived in the United States, offering support and assistance. Their kindness inspired me to live a life of giving.

Every day, I aim to be a charitable person, even if it means volunteering my time or resources. There are a few specific charities that hold a special place in my heart. One of them is directly helping a fire victim back in my home country who suffered severe burns. I assist her by covering the cost of her medication, as accessing medical care and medicine is not as easy back home as it is in the United States. Many people lack the financial means to afford proper healthcare, so I do what I can to support her. In the future, I hope to establish a charity dedicated to helping fire victims in her honor, with the goal of providing assistance to as many individuals as possible.

Another charity that is close to my heart focuses on providing education for young children in my homeland. A few years ago, I started a school back in my country and, although I couldn't physically be there to manage it, I worked extra hours to send money home to support its operations. I would go to places like Walmart and purchase educational games to send back to the children. It brought me great joy to ensure that these children had access to a quality education, even if it required working extra to finance it. Unfortunately, due to the financial challenges posed by the pandemic, I had to temporarily close the school. However, my aspiration is to reopen it someday. In the meantime, I continue to help in any way I can, whether it's assisting those back home or lending a hand to those in need in my new home in Boston.

I want to challenge you to reflect on the last time you extended a helping hand to someone in need. I'm not talking about simply reposting a social media post for awareness, although that is also important. I'm referring to the last time you genuinely provided assistance to someone, even if it seemed like a small gesture to you but made a significant impact on the other person's life.

This book is a reflection of who I am as a person and delves into the reasons that have shaped me into the individual I am today. It unveils my deep love and care for others, a passion that drives me to dedicate my life to serving those in need. I have been recognized by my local newspaper as the "Uber hero," but I want to emphasize that I am just an ordinary man who was raised with a genuine concern for people, regardless of their background or origin.

I don't expect everyone to adopt the same level of commitment to charitable acts of kindness as I have. My intention is simply to encourage people to make genuine connections with one another, to empathize with their experiences, and perhaps inspire them to show empathy and compassion in their own unique way. You don't have to go to extreme lengths like I have. Small acts of kindness can make a significant difference.

In the pages of this book, you will find multiple accounts of occasions where I risked my own life to save others. But it's important to note that not everyone is expected to do the same. My belief is that helping people is an inherent part of my purpose in life. What I'm asking of you, the reader, is to demonstrate small acts of kindness in your own life. Take moments to put down your phones, truly connect with your fellow human beings, and engage in meaningful conversations. Through these actions, you can extend a helping hand whenever the opportunity arises, creating a positive impact in the lives of others.

CHAPTER 2

PURPOSE

In the realm of my origins, you'll find,
The roots that shaped my heart and mind.
From Guinea West Africa's land, I hail with pride,
A humble soul on a selfless ride.

The CBS News bestowed upon me a name,
The Uber hero, they proclaimed.
Though flattered, I remain just a simple man ,
A man with love and kindness embedded.

My mission, clichéd as it may sound,
Is to make this world a better ground.
With empathy, concern, and open arms,
I strive to soothe the world's weary qualms.

For I truly believe in the power of love,
Sent forth to heal, like a gentle dove.
Regardless of acquaintance or knowing,
Respect and warmth I am always bestowing.

A shirt off my back, I'd offer with grace,
To anyone in need, any time, any place.
The people's welfare, my compass, my guide,
For within their hearts, our unity resides.

So let not the titles or accolades define,
The essence of who I am in this rhyme.
Call me Mohammed, a beacon of light,
An Uber hero, embracing love's might.

Allow me to introduce myself. My name is Mohamed Sanusie Traore born on March 4, 1982, in Guinea West Africa. Today, I now reside in Boston, MA As I sit here reflecting on my life, I can't help but feel a sense of awe and pride as I witness the world taking notice of my story. The news reporter shared my tale, and at that moment, I was overwhelmed with emotions. However, it wasn't just personal pride that engulfed me; I wished my family could have been present to witness this honorable moment. They are the ones who instilled in me the values that led me down this path.

I think back to the day I saw the news reporter, and I remember feeling shocked. But although I was proud I longed for my family to witness this momentous occasion. They are the ones who taught me the importance of empathy and selflessness. Growing up in a family of seven siblings, our household was always filled with love and compassion. We shared everything—our rooms, clothes, food, toys—and most significantly, our parents. They weren't just parents to us; they became parents to anyone who needed their love and care.

As a child, I must admit, it wasn't always easy to constantly share my space with other families. There were moments when I felt annoyed or inconvenienced by the constant stream of people coming in and out of our home. But I couldn't voice those frustrations because my mother taught us the importance of selflessness and compassion. It was an integral part of who she was, and she nurtured the same qualities within us, her children.

Helping others became the core of my existence. It was ingrained in me, not just through words, but through the actions of my parents. They showed me the profound joy that comes from giving selflessly to others. Their lessons shaped me into the person I am today, and I carry their legacy with me.

Fast forward to the day, I witnessed a family in desperate need of help. The news reporter described me as a hero when sharing the story, but to me, it felt like second nature. I didn't consider myself a hero, nor did I think about the dangers I was putting myself in. I simply acted on the values instilled in me since childhood. I couldn't bear to see someone suffer without finding a way to lend a hand.

To truly comprehend the significance of this story, it is important to delve into who I am as a person and the upbringing that shaped me. Growing up, I was one of seven siblings, the second youngest among us. Our family possessed a remarkable sense of charity and benevolence that permeated every aspect of our lives.

As an African immigrant in America, my charitable endeavors have expanded to encompass both my homeland and the people I encounter randomly in this country. Every day, as I drive for Uber, I have the opportunity to connect with individuals from diverse backgrounds. Some are burdened by their struggles, while others simply need someone to listen or a small act of kindness. In those moments, I seize the chance to brighten their day and remind them that they are not alone.

But as I continue on this journey, I can't help but ponder the impact my dedication to helping others has on my own family, particularly my son who remains in Africa. I hope he understands that everything I do is driven by a deep love for him and a genuine desire to create a better world for him and future generations. I want him to know the incredible impact that a single act of kindness can have on someone's life and to carry that compassion with him as he grows. I am the type of person I am today by watching my mom and dad offering anything they had to help others. I hope one day my son will learn from my acts of kindness and my charitable giving also rub off on him.

Reflecting on my life's journey, I am struck by the interconnectedness of our world. Acts of kindness have the power to ripple across continents, transcending borders and cultural barriers. The outpouring of support and love I have received from people who may have never met my mother but know of her legacy through me and my siblings is a testament to the enduring impact of goodness.

As I navigate through life, driven by the principles instilled in me by my mother, I strive to be a source of light in a world that sometimes feels overshadowed by darkness. I will continue to lend a helping hand, be there for those in need, and spread love and compassion wherever I go. In honoring my mother's memory and carrying on her legacy, I find purpose, fulfillment, and the undeniable joy that comes from making a difference in the lives of others.

Being an African immigrant in America has given my charitable endeavors a broader scope. While I remain connected to my homeland and strive to make a difference there, I also encounter countless opportunities to extend a helping hand to strangers in the United States. Every day, as I drive my Uber, I meet people from various walks of life. Some are burdened by their struggles, others are simply in need of a listening ear or a small act of kindness. In those moments, I seize the opportunity to brighten someone's day, to offer support, and to remind them that they are not alone.

I often ponder how my actions impact my own family, particularly my son who resides in Africa. Does he ever feel neglected or overshadowed by the constant demands of my philanthropic pursuits? I hope not. I hope he understands that the driving force behind my commitment to helping others is rooted in love and the desire to create a better world for him and generations to come. I want him to witness the profound impact that a single act of kindness can have on someone's life and to carry that understanding with him as he grows.

Continuing this journey, I am grateful for the lessons my mother taught me. She showed me that true happiness lies not in accumulating material possessions but in the profound joy that comes from giving selflessly to others. And now, as I put my mother to rest, I am proud of the way people are celebrating her life and the way they have stepped up to support me and my siblings during this difficult time. It is a testament to the love and compassion that she embodied and passed down to us.

In this interconnected world, where acts of kindness can ripple across continents, I am humbled by the outpouring of support and love I have received from people who may have never met my mother but know of her legacy through me and my siblings. It reinforces the power of goodness, the impact we can have on one another, and the lasting impression we can leave behind.

As I navigate through life, driven by the principles instilled in me by my mother, I strive to be a source of light in a world that sometimes feels overshadowed by darkness. I will continue to lend a helping hand, be there for those in need, and spread love and compassion wherever I go. In honoring my mother's memory and carrying on her legacy, I find purpose, fulfillment, and the undeniable joy that comes from making a difference in the lives of others

CHAPTER 3

A DAY I WILL NEVER FORGET

Dear Uber,

I am writing this letter with utmost sincerity to bring to your attention an extraordinary incident that unfolded during one of my rides as an Uber driver. I believe you must know that there are remarkable individuals in your driver community who go above and beyond to make a positive impact, despite the negative stories that often dominate the headlines.

As an immigrant from Guinea West Africa, I have embraced the opportunities that Uber has provided me, enabling me to not only earn a living but also contribute to the well-being of those I encounter. I take immense pride in being a part of this platform and the positive change it can bring to our communities.

Recently, during one of my routine rides in Boston, I stumbled upon a scene that would forever stay etched in my memory. I witnessed a family in desperate need of assistance, yet surrounded by bystanders who seemed more interested in capturing the moment on their smartphones than offering a helping hand.

Without hesitation, I sprang into action. It was as if an invisible force guided me to prioritize human life over anything else. I understood that this was a pivotal moment, a chance to make a difference in the lives of those who needed it the most. With a surge of adrenaline, I approached the distressed family and offered my support.

The gravity of the situation unfolded before my eyes. The family was facing a dire circumstance, and their well-being depended on someone stepping in and extending a helping hand. While others chose to remain passive observers, I embraced the spirit of compassion and empathy that has been instilled in me since childhood.

At that moment, I embodied the essence of a hero. It wasn't about seeking recognition or personal gain; it was a genuine desire to make a positive impact in someone's life. I did what any compassionate human being would do in the face of adversity – I extended my assistance to those in need.

It is disheartening to witness how negative news stories often overshadow the countless acts of kindness and heroism performed by Uber drivers every day. These stories go untold, leaving a void in the perception of your company and its dedicated drivers. I urge you, Uber, to shed light on the remarkable deeds that take place within your community.

By acknowledging and celebrating the selfless acts of drivers, you have the power to shift the narrative and restore faith in the hearts of riders and drivers alike. It is through these stories that the true essence of Uber can be revealed – a platform that connects individuals with compassion and promotes positive change in our society.

I write this letter not only to express my personal experience but also on behalf of the countless unsung heroes who share the same commitment to helping others. These drivers embody the values that Uber stands for and are a testament to the positive impact your platform can have on communities around the world.

Thank you for taking the time to read this letter and for considering the importance of recognizing the extraordinary efforts of Uber drivers. Together, we can showcase the incredible acts of compassion and kindness that occur daily, spreading a message of hope and inspiring others to embrace the power of empathy.

Sincerely,

Mohamed Sanusie Traore

A DAY I NEVER FORGET

It was around 9:30 at night when I witnessed a life-changing event. My day had been ordinary, just like any other. I had decided to take a few rides as an Uber driver before heading home. Little did I know that on that particular day, I would find myself risking my own life to save two others.

As fate would have it, I found myself in the vicinity of the accident. I had just dropped off a passenger on that side of town when I received another ride request to the opposite side. However, something inside me made me cancel that ride. I decided not to go to that part of town. Instead, I accepted a ride from the airport, which would eventually lead me to the site of the accident. Looking back, it felt as though the universe had a hand in guiding me there.

The airport ride was a lucrative one, a $50 fare from the airport to Summerville As an Uber driver, such fares are essential for our earnings. With the fare accepted, I began making my way to pick up the passenger. It was around 9:30 when I spotted a vehicle flipped over on the side of the highway. The rain made the weather treacherous, and there was no sign of police or ambulances yet.

My heart couldn't ignore the scene unfolding before me. People were driving past, completely oblivious to the fact that someone might be in desperate need of help. I couldn't stand idly by. I made a decision to pull over on the opposite side of the street and brave the busy road to investigate if anyone was inside the overturned car, hoping I could offer assistance.

As I approached the vehicle, I heard desperate cries for help from a lady trapped inside. She had been screaming for a while, and her voice was growing weaker by the minute. It was disheartening to see her feeling defeated. The car was still running, and there was a dangerous leakage of some unknown fluid. To my surprise, I discovered a 6-year-old girl was also trapped inside. The situation was dire.

Breaking the glass to free them crossed my mind initially, but I realized it could cause more harm than good. I observed the lady struggling to push the door open, but it was too heavy for her. I looked around, hoping for assistance, but no one seemed willing to step forward. With no one else to rely on, I summoned every ounce of strength within me and managed to lift the door somehow, even though I can't explain how.

I held the door up, and the lady managed to push her daughter's head out of the car. The girl was halfway in and halfway out, which terrified me. I knew I couldn't hold the heavy door for long, and the situation was growing increasingly dangerous. Frantically, I called out for help, hoping someone would step up and assist. Unfortunately, people merely stood by, capturing videos on their phones, showing no intention of lending a hand. The gravity of the situation weighed heavily on me.

Realizing that time was running out, I had to act quickly. Determined, I used all my might to push the door with my right hand, straining under its weight. Miraculously, I lifted the door and managed to pull the child out completely using my right hand. I repeated the same for the mother, defying my own limitations. To this day, I'm amazed at how I found the strength to do it.

Once they were safely away from the car, which continued to leak fluids, a sense of relief washed over me. Just moments later, the vehicle became engulfed in smoke, highlighting the severity of the situation. More people began arriving, causing traffic to pile up. Fire trucks and police were dispatched to the scene, and thankfully, we were already out of harm's way when a loud explosion shook the area. It happened in Revere, Massachusetts, near Boston, and the incident attracted attention from those nearby.

The growing crowd prevented people from getting too close to the burning car, as it posed a significant danger. I consider myself fortunate to have rescued the lady and her daughter in the nick of time. The police took my name and contact information, and I provided them with a detailed account of what had transpired. They commended me as a hero. The paramedics offered to take me to the hospital, concerned about my injured shoulder, but I decided to go the next day instead.

Exhausted yet filled with pride, I drove home, grateful to have made a difference. After a refreshing shower, I stopped by the local CVS to purchase

Bengay for my sprained shoulder. The following day, I received an unexpected call from the chief of police, expressing his gratitude. He had seen the entire incident captured on camera. The news channel even picked up the story, referring to me as the "Uber Hero." It was a headline I never anticipated but one that filled me with a sense of accomplishment

One thing that weighs on my heart is the fact that I never had the chance to reconnect with the family after the incident. I didn't have their contact information, so I couldn't reach out to them. I understand that they might prefer to put that day behind them, but I often think about them and hope that they haven't suffered too much from the traumatic experience. I particularly worry about the lasting impact it may have had on the little girl, as trauma can lead to various forms of anxiety.

As for myself, I did experience a couple of nightmares in the immediate aftermath, but overall, I am doing fine. It was an extremely traumatic experience, but I would willingly go through it again if it meant saving lives. I sincerely hope that the family is doing well and that they have been able to move forward from that harrowing incident. We were all incredibly fortunate to have survived, considering the potential explosion that could have occurred while I was trying to extricate them from the car. If only a few minutes had passed, the outcome could have been vastly different. I firmly believe that I was meant to be there at that precise moment in time, and I am proud of myself for taking action and making a difference.

My actions serve as a testament to the belief that every person can make a positive impact. It's about being there for others, extending a hand when it's needed, and showing that we care. Through these small acts of kindness, we can create a ripple effect that inspires others to do the same.

While being called a hero may be flattering, I see myself as an ordinary person who is driven by a deep love for others. I find fulfillment in knowing that I can make a difference, no matter how small, and that my actions may inspire someone else to do the same. It's not about seeking glory or validation; it's about being true to who I am and living a life guided by compassion and empathy.

A moment that filled me with immense pride was when my home country in Guinea West Africa, Guinea, honored me for my actions. They showcased my achievements on their website and highlighted the coverage I received from CBS News in the United States. The recognition and support from my country made me feel deeply appreciated and valued. It was a special moment for me, and my mom, in particular, was bursting with pride. She saw in me a reflection of the values she instilled in me as I grew up.

I witnessed my mother consistently embodying compassion and kindness towards others, serving as a role model for me. Her example inspired me to live a life dedicated to helping those in need. I strive to follow in her footsteps, making a positive impact through selfless service. The principles I witnessed my parents embodying throughout my entire life have shaped the person I have become.

I believe that a significant portion of the world lacks empathy for others. Many individuals feel that when someone is in trouble, they are left to fend for themselves. People often become so absorbed in their own lives that they neglect to consider what others may be going through. This saddens me deeply. I genuinely wish that people would show more kindness towards one another.

My personal mission is to assist those in need through acts of kindness. I have come to realize that the energy we put out into the world often determines the kind of energy we receive in return. Therefore, it is essential to cultivate a positive and compassionate attitude. Being good to others brings about positive outcomes, while negativity breeds negativity. It is my belief that kindness is a force that can make a significant difference in the lives of others and in the world as a whole.

CHAPTER 4
A LEGACY OF KINDNESS;
(HONORING MY MOTHER'S MEMORY)

Seven children she raised with utmost grace,
A responsibility daunting, a challenge so grand,
Yet she opened her heart to those in need demand.

Our family, a haven for the less fortunate souls,
Weeks turned to months, and years took their toll.
In our humble abode, other kids found their place,
Fostered by my mother's love, nurtured with her embrace.

Sharing became our virtue, ingrained deep within,
Not just our belongings, but our parents' love to begin.
Though at times, I may have felt uncertain and small,
Now I stand proud, understanding the essence of it all.

As I bid farewell to my mother, tears streaming down,
I find solace in the celebration of her life's renown.
The lives she touched, the hearts she mended,
Her legacy of kindness, forever extended.

In her honor, people from far and wide convene,
To help us lay her to rest, in a somber, sacred scene.
Strangers and friends, united by love's embrace,
Guided by the morals she instilled, a compassionate chase.

In this time of grief, I'm surrounded by love's sweet embrace,
From Africa to the United States, a testament to her grace.
Though my heart aches, I'm filled with pride,
For the purpose we share, my mother and I are side by side.

I'm humbled by the love, the support that I receive,
From those who knew her and those who believe,
That the goodness she shared, the light she bestowed,
Lives on in my actions, the seeds she sowed.

No time to truly grieve, for love's abundance is near,
Embracing me, reminding me of why I hold dear,
The mission is to help others, to extend a helping hand,
In honor of my mother's legacy, an eternal command.
So, let us celebrate her life, her spirit so bright,
As I carry her torch, igniting love's radiant light.
A chapter ends, a legacy prevails,
In the kindness we show, in the love that never fails.

Losing a parent is an indescribable pain, one that shakes the very foundation of our being. Throughout my life, my parents were not only my guides but also the epitome of goodness. Their examples taught me how to be a good person, and it is through the process of Laying to rest my mother that I truly understood the impact of people who love and appreciate kindness. The outpouring of love and support from people across the country was a testament to the profound influence my parents had on others. It became clear to me that their legacy of generosity and compassion touched lives far beyond our own. This chapter is dedicated to the memory of my beloved mother and how her acts of charity shaped not only her life but mine as well and my siblings as well.

I had a wonderful childhood growing up with my parents, who were hard working entrepreneurs. They were traders and didn't have much formal education, but their determination was inspiring. They would buy various goods and travel to smaller villages to sell them. Alongside supporting our own family, they also extended their help to other children in need. Our home was always filled with children from different backgrounds. Although my parents didn't officially adopt them, they provided them with food, paid for their school fees, and even offered clothing to assist their families. Witnessing my parents' selflessness and generosity deeply during the war in Sierra Leone impacted me. During the war, which lasted from 1992 to 2001, Our house in Guinea became a refuge for those affected. We opened our doors to around 20 children, offering them a safe place to stay. Despite the challenging circumstances, my mother took it upon herself to care for them, ensuring they had access to education and teaching them valuable skills. Her efforts were remarkable, and though she never received any formal recognition, she was dearly loved by many in the community. These experiences during my childhood shaped my perspective and instilled in me the importance of acts of kindness and compassion.

My parents led a life of selflessness and compassion. Their unwavering dedication to helping others was rooted in their core values. Our home was not just a sanctuary for our own family; it was a haven for countless others. My mother, in particular, had a heart to help children and families in need . Always ready to provide shelter, support, and love to those in need. It was a regular occurrence for our family to share everything we had with others, embracing the belief that true happiness lies in giving to others.

As we gathered to lay my mother to rest, something extraordinary happened. People from different walks of life, whose lives were touched by her kindness, converged to honor her memory. The atmosphere was not one of sadness but of celebration—a celebration of a life lived in service to others. Amidst the pain of loss, we found solace in the stories shared by those whose lives my mother had touched. It was a reminder of the vast impact a single person can have when driven by love and compassion.

While grieving, I came to realize how much my mother and I were alike. Her legacy of kindness and charity became a beacon that illuminated my path. Each day, I wake up with the question of how I can help others, even in small ways. This behavior was instilled in me from an early age, a testament to the powerful influence of my parents. Their teachings and examples continue to guide me, inspiring me to honor my mother's memory by living a life dedicated to acts of kindness.

It was during the process of laying my mother to rest that the full extent of her impact became evident. Countless individuals came forward with heartfelt stories of how my mother had changed their lives. She had provided shelter, support, and unwavering love to those who needed it most. I was astounded by the sheer number of people who had been touched by her kindness. Each story reaffirmed the importance of empathy, reminding me that even the smallest acts of kindness can leave an indelible mark on someone's life.

The pain of losing my mother remains, her spirit lives on through the values she instilled in me. I am determined to honor her memory by embracing her teachings and continuing her legacy of kindness and charity. Every day presents an opportunity to make a positive impact, extend a helping hand, and bring joy to others. It is through these acts that I keep her spirit alive and ensure that her influence endures.

Losing my mother was the most challenging experience I have ever faced. Yet, during my grief, I witnessed the remarkable impact she had on others. Her selflessness, kindness, and compassion were the cornerstones of her life, and they continue to inspire me. I am forever grateful for the lessons she taught me and the love she shared with the world. By carrying her legacy forward, I hope to honor her memory and inspire others to embrace a life of kindness, compassion, and service to others. I am who I am because of my mother.

CHAPTER 5

CHILDHOOD MEMORIES OF GUINEA WEST AFRICA

When I was a young boy, I was always a peacemaker. I didn't like conflict; I wanted people to be happy. Of course, I was just a normal boy who loved to run around and play, sometimes getting into trouble unintentionally. Being the second youngest among my siblings, I probably got away with more than my older brothers and sisters. The only time I would really get in trouble was for playing too much, jumping, running, knocking things over, and breaking things in the process. It was all part of being a typical boy.

However, my parents always made sure that we were learning something. They instilled in us the importance of studying, even though they themselves never had the opportunity for education. They also taught us practical skills, which they excelled at. Growing up in our village in Guinea west Africa there were no street lights instead, we relied on my parents' trusty flashlight. It was a simple yet essential tool for us.

In the absence of electricity in our village, the flashlight became our guiding light. After school, when the daylight started to fade, we would play outdoors. It would get dark early, and we needed the flashlight to navigate the pitch-black surroundings. The only source of light came from the stars above. My mother would often complain about the batteries in her flashlight because I would frequently borrow it, however, we lived in a town with limited electricity, so we made do with what we had.

Carrying my parents' flashlight became a regular habit for me. My neighbors would laugh and comment on how smart I was for always being prepared. While other kids would run in the dark, I would use the flashlight to light my way. Our neighborhood was relatively safe, so our parents didn't worry too much as long as we stayed close to home. Games like hide and seek became even more thrilling and mysterious in the darkness, with the beam of the flashlight casting eerie shadows.

Those nights spent playing in the dark hold a special place in my heart. It was a time of innocence and adventure, where laughter filled the air. Despite the absence of streetlights, we had the stars and the flashlight we borrowed from our parents to illuminate our childhood memories. They remind me of the joy we found in simple moments, creating bonds of friendship and a sense of togetherness that still bring a smile to my face.

I always been a compassionate child because that's how I was raised. However, there were moments when I couldn't help but feel a twinge of jealousy when my mom dedicated all her time to helping others, especially children in need. As a young child, I longed for my parents' undivided attention, but the constant presence of other kids in our home for whom my mom cared deeply made it difficult.

I couldn't deny the positive influence my parents' kind-heartedness had on me. Their selflessness and generosity slowly seeped into my own being, shaping my values and guiding me towards acts of goodness from an early age. By the time I was around nine or ten years old, I began following in their footsteps, eager to make a difference in my own small way.

I soon discovered that even the simplest acts of kindness held immense power. Whether it was lending a helping hand to an elderly neighbor or lending an ear to a friend in need, I found joy in showing compassion to those around me. These acts became my way of continuing the legacy of love and care instilled in me by my parents.

There was one that left a lasting impression on me when I was around 10 . A funny story . It wasn't funny to me at the time but after a while I couldn't help but to laugh at myself. What I realize is when I was a young boy I made all kinds of silly choices like any other young boy . It's funny who I was back then and who I am now . The innocence of a child but still the core of who i am today

While reading this book, my aim is to make you laugh and cry, to let you know who I am, how I think, and to create a genuine connection. I am who I am because of my upbringing—the encounters I had from childhood to adulthood shaped me into a person who genuinely loves others.

When I was a young boy of about ten years old, I had a neighbor who was around 85 years old. She didn't have any grandchildren, so I would frequently visit her house to help with errands and chores. She enjoyed my company and grew quite fond of me. I was always friendly and helpful to her, and she appreciated it greatly.

As a token of her gratitude, she would often reward me with an egg after I finished assisting her. You might wonder why an egg held such significance. Well, in our community, eggs weren't easy to come by. African eggs, in particular, were smaller due to the natural way chickens were raised, unlike in America where hormones were given to them. So, receiving an egg was a special treat for me, and it brought me great joy.

After each visit, I would rush home with the precious egg in hand, eager for my sister to cook it for me. The anticipation of savoring that egg was unmatched. However, one day, my good deed earned me an unexpected surprise. I had been particularly helpful to my elderly neighbor, and she was delighted. In appreciation, she gave me not one, but three eggs—a remarkable reward for my efforts.

I held the three eggs in my hands, feeling a sense of pride. She advised me to go straight home and carefully store the eggs to prevent any cracks. But my excitement and desire to share my good fortune got the best of me.

Instead of following her advice, I set off to find my best friend, eager to share one of the eggs with him. It was an act of friendship and the joy of sharing. Holding one egg in my left hand, another in my right, I placed the third egg in my pocket. However, my innocent ten-year-old mind failed to realize that a pocket wasn't the best place for an egg.

With excitement bubbling inside me, I finally reached my best friend to deliver the news of my good deed and the three eggs I had earned. But when I reached into my pocket to retrieve the third egg, disappointment struck. The fragile shell had cracked, creating a mess within my pocket. At that moment, I was a mix of emotions—upset, frustrated, and unable to find the humor in the situation.

I shared my mishap with my friend, expressing my disappointment that my intention to share had been foiled by my own foolishness. While he found it amusing, I struggled to see the funny side at that particular time. He playfully questioned why I would put an egg in my pocket, reminding me that eggs don't belong there. It was a stark reminder of my own carelessness and lack of foresight.

Looking back on this memory, it now brings a smile to my face. It's a testament to the innocence and laughter of childhood, even amidst the lessons learned. The story highlights the importance of not taking ourselves too seriously and finding humor in our own mistakes. So, as I reflect on that day, I can't help but laugh at my youthful antics and the cracked egg that taught me a valuable lesson.

I didn't like fighting with anyone when I was a kid . I guess I have the same personality. I was just younger. Still today I don't like arguing and fighting .

One of the simple joys of our childhood was catching crickets. It became a fun game for us, always competing to see who could find the most crickets. We would spend hours chasing after them, giggling with delight. But there was one incident that I vividly remember, a day that took a surprising turn.

I was determined to catch a particular cricket that had cleverly hopped into a hole. Unfortunately, none of us had anything to dig with except for my friend. I managed to convince him to lend me his digging tool while I tried to unearth the elusive cricket. With great enthusiasm, he began digging, thrusting his hand into the hole to retrieve the cricket for me. To our shock, he ended up grasping something entirely different—a snake!

In an instant, panic ensued. We all scattered in fear, running as fast as our legs could carry us. Amidst the chaos, the guy whose hand had encountered the snake became furious with me. He blamed me for putting him in harm's way and vowed to teach me a lesson. From that day forward, whenever he saw me, he would attempt to confront and fight me.

However, fighting was not in my nature. Even at a young age, I was a peacemaker. I disliked conflicts and believed in finding peaceful resolutions. So, instead of engaging in a physical altercation, I confronted him with a different approach. During one of his pursuits, as he chased me, I mustered the courage to speak up. I warned him that if he continued to bully and harass me, I would report his behavior to his parents.

It was a bold move, but I knew deep down that he understood right from wrong. Our parents had repeatedly cautioned us about the dangers of putting our hands into holes. He was well aware of the rule, despite my plea for his assistance in catching the cricket. I made it clear to him that if he persisted in his attempts to harm me, I would inform his parents about his reckless action, regardless of its forbidden nature.

Surprisingly, my words struck a chord within him. He realized the consequences of his actions and the potential repercussions from his parents. Gradually, his harassment ceased, and he stopped pursuing me. The power of peaceful resolution had prevailed, and I no longer had to fear his wrath.

Looking back, that incident taught me the value of finding nonviolent solutions, even in the face of adversity. It reinforced my belief in the importance of peacekeeping and seeking understanding rather than resorting to aggression. The encounter with the snake became a turning point, allowing me to assert my own strength through words and diffusing conflict. It was a valuable lesson that would shape my approach to conflicts throughout my life.

Growing up with seven siblings, conflict was inevitable. However, compared to some of my friends and their siblings, our fights were relatively few and far between. We were a close-knit bunch, but like any family, we had our moments of bickering. Despite my aversion to conflict, I learned that disagreements were an inherent part of having a large family.

I particularly recall the playful back-and-forth I had with my brother, who was close in age to me. Our childhood home was illuminated by candles and kerosene lamps, as electricity was a luxury we didn't have at that time. One day, while engrossed in our usual antics, we were jumping on the bed when an unfortunate accident occurred. My brother accidentally knocked over and broke a lamp.

Panic ensued as we realized the consequences of our actions. In that moment, my brother pleaded with me not to tell our parents, hoping to avoid the punishment that would surely follow. However, I firmly believed in honesty and knew that confessing the truth was the right thing to do. I couldn't bear the weight of hiding the incident from our parents.

Resolute in my decision, I assured my brother that I had to tell our parents the truth. He reluctantly accepted my stance and left the room while I began cleaning up the broken lamp. Little did I know at the time, he had a clever plan in mind. Unbeknownst to me, he decided to turn the tables on me, knowing that I intended to inform our parents about the mishap.

To my surprise, my brother took the initiative and went straight to our father, confessing that I was the one responsible for breaking the lamp. I was dumbfounded by his betrayal, as I had trusted his understanding of the importance of honesty. Nevertheless, my father, unaware of the truth, reprimanded me and imposed a punishment for my supposed actions.

In a family with multiple siblings, even the most peaceful among us can find themselves caught up in disputes. It was a reminder that conflict is an inherent part of growing up with siblings. Despite my efforts to maintain harmony, there were still moments of disagreement and discord.

Reflecting on my childhood, I can't help but smile. Yes, I witnessed and understood a lot at an early age due to the circumstances of war and my parents' compassionate actions. I observed them caring for the less fortunate, but I also had my fair share of simple joys and carefree moments. I reveled in being a boy, running and playing with my siblings, and cherishing the beauty of our humble upbringing.

These humble beginnings shaped who I am as a man today. They instilled in me a deep appreciation for the simple pleasures of life and the value of honesty, even in the face of sibling rivalries. While conflicts may arise, it is through these experiences that we grow, learn, and forge unbreakable bonds with those closest to us.

Man pulls woman, child from burning car in Revere

A good Samaritan rescued a mother and her child after a fiery crash. WBZ-TV's Mike Sullivan reports.

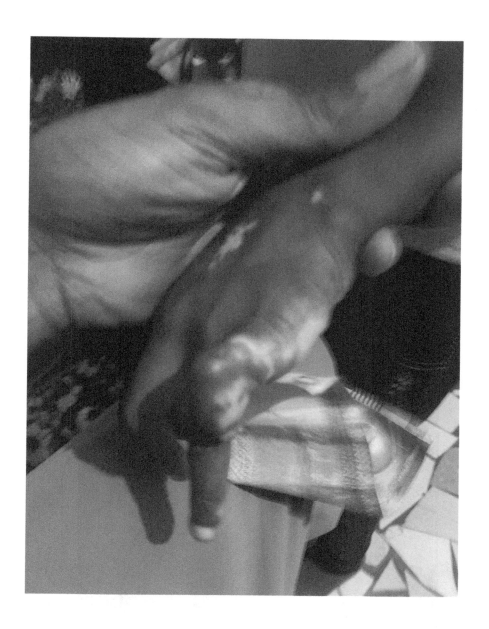

CHAPTER 6

A WORLD OF COMPASSION

In a world where compassion is in dire need,
Where hearts ache for empathy to succeed,
Let us pause, reflect, and heed the call,
To extend our hands to those who may fall.

When was the last time we lent a helping hand,
Fed the hungry or helped them understand,
That is a world that can be harsh and cold,
Acts of kindness are worth more than gold?

Have we walked the streets where the homeless reside,
Shared a meal, listened to their stories, side by side?
Or have we turned a blind eye, sealed our hearts,
As they endure the world's merciless darts?

When we pass by someone burdened with despair,
Do we stop and offer solace, showing we care?
Or do we simply walk past, lost in our haste,
Ignoring their suffering, their pain left untraced?

Where is the respect for the human soul,
The reverence that makes us whole?
Let us ponder these questions, deep and true,
And contemplate what it means to be human too.

For within each of us lies the power to heal,
To bridge divides and understand what others feel,
It's in the small gestures, the acts of grace,
That we can brighten someone's weary face.

A simple seat offered to an elder's frame,
A hand to hold, easing their journey's claim,
A kind word spoken to lift a burdened spirit,
Can make a world of difference, let's not forget it.

The measure of a person goes far beyond,
The material wealth or titles they have donned,
It lies in the depth of their compassion's reach,
In the lives they touch, and the lessons they teach.

So let us strive to be better than we were,
To wipe away tears, help dreams to occur,
With empathy as our guiding star above,
Together, we'll create a world ablaze with love.

Let's build shelters for the homeless to find rest,
Support the vulnerable and give them their best,
Volunteer at hospitals, lend a listening ear,
To those fighting battles, overwhelmed by fear.

Let's weave a tapestry of compassion's threads,
Engage in acts of kindness, where humanity spreads,
For it is in our unity that we truly shine,
And make this world a better place, divine.

So, my fellow beings, let's rise and ignite,
The flame of empathy, burning ever bright,
For in the depths of our hearts, we hold the key,
To unlock the door to a world where love is free.

A World of Compassion

As I returned home to bury my beloved mother, little did I know that the journey would lead me to a life-altering encounter, forever etching a tale of compassion into the fabric of my being. Amidst the weight of grief and the somber purpose that brought me back to my homeland, I found myself crossing paths with a mother and her young daughter—a moment that would redefine my understanding of empathy and reshape the course of my life. In this chapter, I share the raw and unfiltered account of this extraordinary experience, a true testament to the universal need for compassion and our shared responsibility to create a world where empathy thrives. The journey back to my hometown was tinged with a bittersweet mixture of nostalgia and sorrow. The familiar streets seemed to whisper stories of my mother's love and the memories we had woven together. It was during this pilgrimage of remembrance that fate interweaved its delicate threads, guiding me towards an unexpected path—one that would soon intersect with the lives of a mother and her young daughter, forever changing the course of our destinies.

As I made my way to visit my sister, I noticed a gathering commotion on the bustling street. Intrigued, I was drawn toward the epicenter of the chaos. To my utter dismay, I was confronted with a heartbreaking sight—an 11-year-old girl, her delicate frame wilting under the weight of illness, teetering on the precipice of collapse. The scorching heat mercilessly pressed down upon her frail shoulders, exacerbating her condition until she succumbed, falling onto the unforgiving asphalt. The anguish of the scene was compounded by the collective apathy that engulfed those witnessing this young life hanging in the balance. Instead of rushing to her aid, a chorus of outstretched arms clutching smartphones emerged, capturing the unfolding tragedy with disturbing detachment. It was a moment that tore through the veneer of humanity and exposed a profound crisis—a crisis of empathy that gripped our world with alarming force.

In that pivotal moment, a lot of emotions swept through me—a potent blend of grief, anger, and an unyielding determination to break the chains of indifference. The essence of my purpose crystallized before me, transcending personal loss and embracing a higher calling—a calling rooted in empathy and selflessness.

Driven by an irrepressible urge to alleviate the suffering before me, I approached the distraught mother, my heart heavy with the weight of her anguish. Seeking reassurance of the girl's condition, I asked if she suffered from any contagious illnesses, a gesture intended to protect both the vulnerable child and myself. Receiving a negative response, I offered what little relief I could muster—a cool trickle of water to quench the girl's parched throat and soothe her fevered brow.

My commitment to compassion did not waver there. Despite the enormity of the task before me, burying my mother and bidding her a final farewell, I knew that I had been entrusted with a profound responsibility. The resolve within me burned brightly, fueled by a deep-seated belief that every act of kindness, no matter how small, held the power to reshape our world.

With urgency in my heart, I extended an offer to the mother—a proposition to transport them to the nearby clinic where the young girl could receive the vital medical attention she so desperately needed. It was a gesture born from a place of profound empathy, an unspoken vow to stand alongside them in their hour of need. Grateful, the mother and daughter accepted my offer, and together, we embarked on a journey of hope, propelled by the transformative force of compassion.

Driving to the hospital with the lady and her sick daughter, My car propelling us forward on that serpentine road, I couldn't help but reflect on the world that lay beyond our immediate reality. The incident I had just witnessed was not an isolated incident; it was a microcosm of a global affliction. The absence of empathy, and the prevalence of indifference—it was a universal struggle that transcended geographical boundaries. My experience that day, interwoven with the tapestry of countless others who had turned their backs on those in need, impelled me to confront the harsh reality that the very fabric of our society was unraveling. I witnessed in my country what I had been seeing in the United States. People no longer cared about helping one another. It saddened me to my core and just made me want to continue to help as many people as I could. I'm only one person so I know that I eventually will need to start some kind of organization, but I am learning it will have to be nationwide. Here I'm supposed to be back in my country to lay my mother to rest and I just happened to run into a family in need.

Arriving at the clinic, I shouldered the weight of responsibility, not only for the lives entrusted to my care but also for the countless others whose cries for compassion had gone unanswered. It was within the sterile walls of that sanctuary of healing that I witnessed the transformative power of empathy firsthand—a glimmer of light in an otherwise darkened world. As I guided the mother and daughter through the labyrinthine corridors, I glimpsed flickers of hope illuminating the faces of weary patients and harried medical professionals.

In a gesture of solidarity, I reached into my pocket, retrieving a handful of crumpled bills—a meager sum in the grand tapestry of worldly wealth, but a lifeline for a family grappling with the harsh realities of poverty. Placing the money into the mother's outstretched hand, I hoped that it would alleviate the burden they bore, if only for a fleeting moment. It was a small act of compassion, a humble offering that held the potential to ignite a ripple of change, both within their lives and within the depths of my soul.

In the aftermath of that profound encounter, as I laid my mother to rest and bid her a final farewell, I carried with me an unwavering resolve—a conviction that compassion was not merely a choice but a moral imperative. The incident had unveiled a purpose that was larger than me, compelling me to become an instrument of empathy in a world thirsting for compassion. It was a calling I could no longer ignore—a call to champion the cause of humanity, to rewrite the narrative of indifference, and to sow seeds of kindness wherever my footsteps led.

Standing before my mother's grave, I vowed to honor her memory by dedicating my life to a world where empathy flourishes, where no soul is left unaided in moments of despair. For within the depths of tragedy lies the potential for immense transformation—a single act of compassion has the power to heal wounds, bridge divides, and ignite a fire within others to carry the torch of empathy forward.

And so, with a heart brimming with hope and a renewed sense of purpose, I stepped into the world—a world in desperate need of compassion and committed myself to the tireless pursuit of empathy, one encounter at a time.

The weight of grief settles upon the protagonist, the loss of his beloved mother becomes an indelible ache in his heart. Yet, amidst the sorrow, an unexpected wave of love and support washes over him from every corner of the globe. Messages of solace, heartfelt calls, and even financial contributions flood in, not solely from those familiar with his mother, but from strangers who were moved by the kindness and empathy exhibited by him and his siblings throughout their lives.

In the wake of my mother's passing, my heart shattered into a thousand pieces. The pain was unbearable, and I felt lost in a world devoid of her warmth and guidance. Yet, as I navigated the depths of my grief, something remarkable began to unfold—a testament to the profound impact my mother had on the lives she touched.

Messages of condolences, calls from distant relatives, and even financial support poured in from every corner of the world. The outpouring of love and compassion was overwhelming, and it became clear that my mother's legacy extended far beyond our immediate family. People who had never met her were moved by the stories they had heard of her selflessness and kindness, and they reached out to offer their support during our darkest hour.

As I received these expressions of love and care, I couldn't help but reflect on the person I had become. My parents, especially my mother, had raised me to be empathetic and compassionate. They instilled in me the values of giving back and helping others in need. And now, in my time of need, I witnessed the true power of those teachings.

The support I received wasn't just a result of people sympathizing with my loss; it was a reflection of the kind of person I had become. Throughout my life, I had tried to follow in my mother's footsteps, extending a helping hand whenever I could. I had witnessed the impact of small acts of kindness and the way they could brighten someone's day. Little did I know that these actions would leave an indelible mark on others and would come back to me when I needed it most.

Amid my grief, I found solace in the knowledge that my mother's legacy was alive within me. I carried her spirit of love and compassion, and it resonated with those who reached out to support me. Their gestures were not merely acts of sympathy; they were a testament to the impact my mother had made on their lives and the way her goodness had rippled out into the world.

The outpouring of love and support became a beacon of light in my darkest days. It reminded me of the power of human connection and the capacity for kindness that exists within each of us. It reinforced my belief that even in a world that often seems cold and detached, empathy and compassion prevail.

While mourning, I made a solemn vow—to honor my mother's memory by continuing to live a life dedicated to helping others. I would carry her torch of compassion and ensure that her legacy of love would endure. The support I received became fuel for this mission, driving me to make a positive impact on the lives of others, just as my mother had done.

In this chapter, I share the profound realization that came from the overwhelming support I received in the aftermath of my mother's passing. It is a testament to the power of love and the enduring impact one person can have on the lives of many. As I carry forward her legacy, I am reminded that the kindness we show to others has the power to shape the world around us and leave a lasting imprint on the hearts of those we touch.

CHAPTER 7

LOVE OVER FEAR

A land consumed by chaos and despair,
A hero emerged, with love and care,
Mohamed, a soul brave and strong,
Embarked on a journey that would right a wrong.

Through war-torn streets, he walked alone,
His heart filled with purpose, his spirit shone,
To rescue his grandmother, in need of aid,
He braved danger's path, undeterred, unswayed.

Amidst the rubble, he found her, weak,
Laying in waste, her voice unable to speak,
With tender hands, he lifted her from despair,
A silent promise formed an unspoken prayer.

Together they stayed, through the fearful night,

Gunshots echoed, casting shadows of fright,

But love wrapped them in its warm embrace,

Their souls intertwined, finding solace and grace.

In whispers and glances, their bond grew strong,

Their spirits entwined, where they both belong,

He became her rock, her pillar of strength,

She became his guiding light, his heart's true wavelength.

Stories were shared, creating memories anew,

Laughter and tears, a testament to love true,

For in that fleeting moment, their hearts understood,

That amidst chaos and fear, love could still intrude.

As days turned to years, their relationship thrived,

Grandmother's heart filled with gratitude revived,

She bestowed upon him gifts of love and care,

A cherished connection that they both would bear.

For in that act of rescue, a bond was sealed,

A tale of love and courage, forever revealed,

This poem, a tribute to their journey untold,

Of a hero and his grandmother, a tale so bold.

May their story inspire, touch hearts far and wide,

With its essence of love, forever abiding,

For in the depths of darkness, they found the light,

A bond unbreakable, shining ever so bright.

Coming to the rescue of the family in the car wasn't the first time I had been faced with a life-or-death situation. It was reminiscent of an experience in my home country when I was much younger, where I found myself risking everything to save my beloved grandmother during a time of immense hardship.

Amidst the chaos of a raging war, my mother had taken my sick grandmother to a hospital in Freetown, Sierra Leone. However, circumstances forced my mother to return to Guinea, leaving my grandmother under the care of our extended family friends. Little did we know that the Rebels would soon invade Freetown, causing everyone to flee for their lives to the other side of the city where it was safe. The Rebels were a very dangerous group and were feared.

The news reached me while I was living in Freetown with my Uncle at the time. The news was that everyone had to flee. When I connected with the family my grandmother was left with:My heart sank as I learned that my grandmother had been left behind. " Your Grandmother is too old to flee. We had to leave her behind. " They told me. I was very upset but I had no time to waste. My Grandmother needed me. Without a moment of hesitation, I decided to go back and find her, regardless of the risks involved. The rebels were ruthless, and being caught by them could end in death. But the love I held for my grandmother and the desire to honor my mother compelled me to embark on a treacherous journey. My mother loved my Grandmother and if her life ended this way she would be devastated.

With determination coursing through my veins, I navigated the war-torn streets of Freetown on foot. The Rebels had burned down most of the vehicles so there were no cars on the road. I walked for 2 hours, barefoot and with fear gripping my heart. The once vibrant city was now a ghost town, with only remnants of its former life scattered among the rubble.

Finally, I arrived at the place where my grandmother had been left behind. The gate was locked, a stark reminder of the chaos that had unfolded. I summoned every ounce of strength within me to climb over it, not knowing what awaited me on the other side.

As I approached the door, a mix of anxiety and hope surged through me. I didn't know if my grandmother was alive or dead, but I was willing to face any danger to find her. With a trembling hand, I tried the doorknob, and to my surprise, it locked. I had to figure out a way to climb up to the second floor and I cautiously stuck my head in the window, my senses on high alert. I was told the Rebels had been on the 3rd floor. If they were still there and I was spotted I would surely die

The house was eerily silent, its walls bearing the scars of the conflict that had ravaged the city. I called out for my grandmother, my voice echoing through the empty rooms. And then, I heard a faint response. Relief flooded over me as I followed her voice, leading me to the room where she was lying. She had lost her voice. She has only been left with water and she was almost out She had been there for 3 days

There she was, my frail grandmother, weak and exhausted. Tears streamed down both our faces as our eyes met. At that moment, the hardships and dangers faded into insignificance. I reassured her that I was there to rescue her from the dire circumstances she had endured.

Overwhelmed with gratitude, my grandmother whispered her thanks, her voice barely audible. She was emaciated and dehydrated, having spent days without sustenance. I frantically searched the house for any provisions, desperately hoping to find something to nourish her. She sat in her waste. She was disabled and couldn't get to the bathroom on her own. I was heartbroken.

She was out of water so I knew the third floor would have supplies because it was where the Rebels were held up for days. I was told they had fled to the mountains but I could have easily run into some of them if I entered the 3rd floor... I had no other choice but to take the risk and go one floor up where my grandmother needed me.

The cost was clear. I discovered a few cans of sardines, biscuits, and bottles of water. It was a meager supply, but it would sustain us for the time being. I gave my grandmother water, helping her rehydrate and regain some strength. The sardines provided a much-needed source of sustenance, and we shared the meager meal in silence. I washed her off and put on her and some fresh clothes as she tried to talk me into leaving. " I'm ok now Grandson but I'm an old woman. I lived a long life but I don't want the Rebels to come back to hurt you... I told her I wouldn't leave without her and I would find a way to get her to the other side of town to safety.

As the night descended, we huddled together, seeking solace and comfort amidst the uncertainty that surrounded us. The distant sound of gunfire served as a constant reminder of the dangers lurking outside. But our bond provided strength and courage, allowing us to find solace in each other's presence.

Throughout the night, we exchanged stories, and memories of happier times that helped to momentarily distract us from the harsh reality unfolding outside. My grandmother's laughter, despite the dire circumstances, filled the room and lifted our spirits. It was a testament to her resilience and indomitable spirit.

As dawn broke, I knew I had to find a way to get my grandmother to safety. I left her in the relative security of the room, promising to return with help. Fortunately, that same day, my mother returned from Guinea, unaware of the perilous situation we had endured.

I devised a plan to relocate my grandmother to the other side of the city, where it was comparatively safer. Luckily I ran into my uncle who came around to see if the Rebels had burned down the buildings. They were known to do that. First, he ran when he first saw me. He thought I was one of the Rebels. I had to call out to him so he knew it was me. With the assistance of my uncle, we managed to escort her through the war-torn streets, avoiding potential dangers along the way. It was a nerve-wracking journey, but the love and determination that fueled us overcame any obstacles we encountered.

Finally, we reached our destination. We met up with some soldiers and told them we need help for my grandmother. They helped us take her to a place where my grandmother could find respite from the horrors of war. The relief and gratitude in my mother's eyes were immeasurable. My grandmother, weak but still filled with gratitude, clung to me, her silent acknowledgment of the immense sacrifice I had made.

In the years that followed, my grandmother's health deteriorated, but her spirit remained unyielding. She passed away peacefully, surrounded by loved ones who cherished her. Her memory lives on, forever etched in our hearts as a symbol of strength, resilience, and the bonds that transcend even the most challenging circumstances.

These experiences have shaped me into the person I am today—a person driven by compassion, empathy, and a deep understanding of the value of life. They serve as a constant reminder of the extraordinary acts of heroism performed by ordinary individuals during times of adversity.

In sharing this story, I hope to shed light on the resilience of the human spirit and the unwavering power of love. It is a testament to the extraordinary lengths we would go to protect and save those we hold dear.

The war eventually came to an end, bringing a fragile peace to the war-torn land. The scars of the conflict would forever remain, etched not only on the physical landscape but also in the hearts and minds of those who lived through it.

Reflecting on those challenging times, I am filled with a profound sense of gratitude and humility. The experiences I had during the war and the courage it took to rescue my grandmother have shaped me in ways I could never have imagined.

The lessons I learned from my mother and grandmother, about compassion, selflessness, and the importance of helping others, continue to guide my actions to this day. Their unwavering love and sacrifice inspire me to be a force for good in the world and to extend a helping hand to those in need, regardless of their background or circumstances.

I have carried these values with me as I journeyed to America as an African immigrant. While building a new life in a foreign land, my commitment to helping people back home in Africa remains steadfast. It is a deep-rooted responsibility, an integral part of who I am.

But it is not only in my homeland that I encounter those in need. In the United States, I come across strangers who could benefit from a helping hand. Whether it is offering support to a struggling neighbor, volunteering at local charities, or engaging in community initiatives, I strive to make a positive difference wherever I go.

There are moments when the weight of my charitable endeavors weighs heavy on my family. My son, living back in Africa, may wonder why I dedicate so much time and energy to helping others. I understand his perspective, for I too once grappled with similar thoughts as a child. Yet, I trust that as he grows older, he will come to appreciate the importance of compassion and service.

The sacrifices we make for the well-being of others may not always be understood or appreciated in the present moment. However, it is the impact we have on the lives of those we touch that truly matters. The legacy of my mother and grandmother lives on through the countless lives they touched, and I strive to honor their memory by continuing their legacy of compassion and generosity.

As I navigate this journey of life, I often reflect on the path that brought me here. From rescuing my grandmother during the war to embracing the values instilled in me by my family, each experience has shaped me into the person I am today.

I am reminded that heroism isn't defined by grand gestures alone but can be found in the small acts of kindness we extend to others. It is in the willingness to put ourselves at risk, to step outside our comfort zones, and to lend a helping hand to those in need.

I hope to inspire others to embrace compassion, seek opportunities to make a positive impact, and recognize the immense power of our actions, no matter how small they may seem.

Together, let us continue to create a world where empathy, love, and selflessness prevail, a world where every individual, regardless of their circumstances, can find solace and support in the outstretched arms of their fellow human beings.

This book is just the first part of my plan to build a group of people who will help me help other people. There's only so much I can do by myself. I know there are still some good people in this world who still have empathy and compassion for other people.

CHAPTER 8

GROWTH AND DREAMS

From distant lands, I journeyed far,
Leaving behind my native shores, a memoir,
Seeking dreams and a future bright,
In a land where possibilities take flight.

America, a land of hope and dreams,
Where the impossible gleams,
I am an immigrant, grateful and proud,
To walk its streets, to stand unbowed.

At first, a culture shock embraced my soul,
Feeling lonely, my heart took its toll,
But in this foreign land, I found my way,
New friends turned family, they helped me sway.

Though oceans separate me from kin so dear,
Their love and presence, forever near,
With every step, I carry their dreams,
To build bridges of hope, where love redeems.

I don't take for granted this land's embrace,
The opportunities it offers, the chance to chase,
A life I've dreamt of, a destiny I mold,
A story of resilience, bravely untold.

United States, a land of endless possibilities,
Where compassion and diversity find unity,
I take it seriously, my duty to give back,
To uplift my community, never to slack.

In my heart, I hold my native land,
Guinea West Africa's beauty, where I first began,
The lessons learned, the values ingrained,
In two worlds, my identity was sustained.

This country, now my second home,
Where growth and success freely roam,
With gratitude, I embrace the chance,
To make the world better, one step in advance.

I strive to be a man of worth,
To spread kindness and unearth,
The potential within, the power to ignite,
A beacon of change, shining bright.

In America, I find solace and peace,
A sanctuary where dreams increase,
I am an immigrant, forever grateful,
For the opportunities, for this fate so fateful.

With each passing day, I'll make my stand,
Contributing to the dreams of this land,
For in unity and purpose, we shall find,
A better world, a legacy aligned.

So, let us march forward, hand in hand,
As immigrants and natives, let us understand,
That is the tapestry of diversity we weave,
Lies the strength to heal, the power to believe.

In this great land, I will thrive,
For America, my heart does strive,
To honor my roots, to build anew,
A life that's cherished, a dream come true.

I have accomplished a great deal since moving to the United States, but I cannot deny that the journey has been filled with challenges. In the beginning, I experienced a profound culture shock as I grappled with learning the language and finding suitable employment. Navigating the unfamiliar terrain and learning to fend for myself while missing my family back home proved to be a daunting task. The loneliness that accompanies being far away from home and separated from loved ones weighed heavily on my heart.

However, as time passed, I discovered that the road became somewhat smoother. It was on a city bus that I had a chance encounter with a fellow African. We struck up a conversation and found solace in our shared experiences. A bond blossomed, leading us to make plans to meet up and explore the city together. We decided to acquire bicycles, which not only allowed us to navigate the streets of Boston but also provided an opportunity to deepen our friendship. Through these shared experiences, I gradually familiarized myself with the city and cultivated a sense of belonging.

In my pursuit of stability, I devoted myself to personal growth and diligently worked towards establishing a firm foundation for my life in the United States. I am deeply grateful for the opportunities that have come my way, and I never take them for granted. The knowledge I have gained during my time here has been invaluable. As I acquired new information and honed my skills, I also experienced personal growth. However, amidst all the learning and progress, I have remained steadfast in the core values instilled in me by my parents — to treat others with love and respect. Moreover, I hold onto the belief that if I can assist someone in need, I should do so without hesitation.

This journey has been a testament to my resilience and determination. While the path has been arduous, I recognize the profound impact it has had on shaping the person I am today. I have embraced the opportunities provided by the United States, while also cherishing the lessons learned from my roots in Guinea West Africa. As I continue along this transformative path, I strive to be a beacon of hope and inspiration, exemplifying the strength and gratitude that comes from a multicultural background.

Working long hours and saving my money In 2013, I was able to fulfill my dream of opening a school for the less fortunate in my homeland. Although I couldn't personally run the school due to living in another country, I hired seven dedicated staff members. Every month, I used my own money to pay their salaries and provide supplies, ensuring that the children received proper education and literacy skills. However, after four years, circumstances changed. I lost one of my jobs and could no longer afford to sustain the school. It was a heart-wrenching decision to close it down. Building and running a school back home had always been my goal after moving to America, as I wanted to make a difference in combating illiteracy. My parents, though illiterate themselves, instilled in me the value of hard work. They provided me with an education and a good life, and I wanted to extend that opportunity to others who lacked access to schooling. I named the school after my mother. She was very proud.

When I had to close the school it was emotionally challenging for me. In the beginning, I was proud of my achievement—saving money, renting a building with five bedrooms, and employing two female and five male teachers. Each teacher received a monthly salary of $200, which was considered substantial in my homeland. I financed everything on my own, even purchasing learning computers for the students from Walmart and shipping them to the school. However, without external funding, when I lost my job and had to renew the building lease, I didn't have the means to continue. I had to inform parents to transfer their children to another school. Perhaps if I had reached out for help at the time, I could have kept the school open. Unfortunately, I didn't know many people I could turn to for support.

I aspire to partner with like-minded individuals and open a larger school someday. My vision is to provide not only basic education in reading and writing but also practical skills and trades, with the aim of combating illiteracy in my homeland. This dream holds a special place in my heart, and I am determined not to give up on it. Over the next few years, I will actively work towards making this project a reality. I believe that by joining forces with others who share the same passion for education and community development, we can make a significant impact and bring about positive change. It is through relentless dedication and unwavering commitment that I hope to contribute to ending illiteracy and empowering the people of my homeland.

Additionally, I hope that through my book, I can raise awareness about the issue of illiteracy and inspire others to join in this mission. By sharing my experiences and the challenges I've faced, I aim to ignite a sense of compassion and drive in readers, encouraging them to lend a helping hand. I believe that when people come together with a shared purpose, remarkable things can happen. Together, we can create a ripple effect of positive change, not only in my homeland but also in the lives of those affected by illiteracy around the world. It is my sincerest hope that my book will touch hearts and inspire individuals to take action, making a difference in the lives of others through their support and involvement.

CHAPTER 9

MY UBER ADVENTURES

The realm of Uber drives, an adventure unfolds,
A tapestry of stories, both new and old,
Among the passengers, a diverse array,
Teaching me lessons along the way.

In this bustling world of constant motion,
I've encountered people, each with their own notion,
Some encounters, delightful and bright,
While others challenged my patience's height.

But from each traveler, a nugget I glean,
A valuable insight, a memory to convene,
Through conversations rich with depth,
Or silent moments where energy is kept.

Driving through unexplored neighborhoods fair,
Witnessing scenery beyond compare,
Passengers sharing music, a harmonious find,
Introducing melodies that expand my mind.

Though not every journey is flawless or kind,
I strive to show up, my best self aligned,
Creating an experience, both safe and secure,
Aiming to offer passengers a ride to endure.

To be an Uber driver, a unique role to embrace,
Patience becomes essential in this fast-paced race,
With kindness and understanding, bridges are built,
Smoothly navigating each passenger's tilt.

Through this venture, I've learned of this land,
The United States, its people, diverse and grand,
I've honed the art of communication's grace,
Unlocking connections, bridging space.

This job may not always be easy, it's true,
But I wouldn't trade it for anything, anew,
For as an Uber driver, I discovered much more,
Beyond extra money, blessings I adore.

It's the stories shared, the human connection,
The chance to brighten someone's life's complexion,
In this adventure, I've grown, I've gained,
From each ride, a treasure unexplained.

So as I continue driving, embarking anew,
I'll embrace the lessons, both old and few,
For in the realm of Uber drives, I find,
A gift of experiences, priceless and kind.

Despite some negative headlines in the past, it's important to recognize that there are many genuinely good people who drive for Uber. These individuals simply want to earn an honest living while enjoying the cities they operate in and meeting new people. I consider myself one of those people who truly loves engaging with others and providing them with an entertaining experience. I strive to brighten people's days with a smile and treat them with respect.

Being an Uber driver has also taught me the value of patience, which is another form of kindness. It's something I had to work on in the past, but through this experience, I have learned a great deal. Patience allows me to navigate challenging situations with passengers and ensures that everyone feels respected and heard.

Being an Uber driver has been a transformative journey that has helped me grow as an individual. It has taught me the importance of kindness, respect, and patience, and I am grateful for the lessons learned through this experience.

As an Uber driver, I have the opportunity to encounter a wide range of individuals, each with their own unique characteristics. I have met some genuinely pleasant people with whom I have enjoyed engaging in conversations. On the other hand, there have been times when I've come across individuals who may not be as friendly, but overall, I wouldn't trade this experience for anything. Every day, I get to interact with new people from diverse backgrounds, and this has taught me a great deal about people in the United States.

Driving through the streets of Boston, I have had the privilege of meeting individuals from various cultures and upbringings, truly experiencing the city as a melting pot. Moreover, I've observed the deep love that the people of Boston have for their city, particularly when it comes to their sports teams. You can't tell them anything negative about their beloved teams. Even though dealing with traffic can be exasperating, driving during significant sports events always brings a sense of excitement. During these times, I encounter a multitude of people, some of whom are dressed in their team's memorabilia.

While there are certainly challenges, one of them being drunk passengers, I've had to navigate through arguments among friends or even couples. However, I genuinely feel that these experiences have been instrumental in my personal growth and learning. I've discovered that I have an affinity for connecting with people and providing them with positive energy. A simple smile or a listening ear can make a significant difference, especially when someone is having a bad day and feels like talking about it. Even when confronted with rude passengers who seem to be looking for a fight, I have never returned their negative energy. I remember instances when individuals entered my car with the intention of causing trouble. One such encounter involved a group of young guys who started arguing amongst themselves, and eventually directed their anger towards me over the choice of music. In a calm and composed manner, I asked them about their music preferences, suggesting that we take turns playing songs. Surprisingly, this simple act sparked a conversation, and by the end of the ride, we had bonded over music. Treating people with kindness, even in difficult situations, often makes them reflect on their behavior and realize the goodness within you. While it may not work all the time, being a good person consistently pays off.

I currently have another job, and Uber serves as my part-time gig. However, I have come to acknowledge that this experience has taught me invaluable lessons about people and about myself. I always knew that I had a fondness for people, but being an Uber driver has reinforced my love for engaging with them and providing positive energy. I have encountered individuals who were initially rude or confrontational, but by maintaining a positive attitude, I've managed to diffuse tension and turn those situations around. There have been times when I've stayed in touch with some passengers, and there have been brief encounters that have left a lasting impact on me. In the eyes of those individuals, I will forever be their Uber hero.

Although I have plans for my future that extend beyond being an Uber driver, I will always cherish this job and the significant experiences it has provided me. I cannot say for certain how much longer I will continue driving, but the knowledge and insights I have gained from this role will stay with me forever.

CHAPTER 10

MISTAKEN IDENTITY

A world of mistaken identities, so surreal,
A tale of a good man, his fate to reveal,
Walking the path of honor and grace,
Unaware of the danger he would face.

He journeyed through life with a heart pure,
Spreading kindness, his intentions sure,
Never seeking trouble, always doing good,
Helping others as every good citizen should.

One fateful day, at a Jamaican eatery's door,
A stranger's gaze, cold and eyes full of war,
Mistaken for another, a victim in disguise,
His life hangs in balance, fear in his eyes.

Unknowingly marked by a thug's vengeful glance,
His life endangered, caught in a deadly dance,
But destiny intervened, a moment's delay,
A chance to escape, to live another day.

The stranger approached, fear coursing through veins,
A chilling revelation, a case of mistaken remains,
The gunman, realizing his target was wrong,
Relieved the innocent man of the burden so strongly.

In the aftermath, gratitude filled his heart,
A survivor's tale, a new chapter to start,
He reached out to loved ones, their worry to quell,
A reminder of the dangers that life can compel.

For even in goodness, shadows may appear,
Testing our courage, instilling a deep-rooted fear,
Yet through it all, he remained steadfast and strong,
A testament to resilience when things go wrong.

In this tale of mistaken identity's plight,
We find courage, compassion shining bright,
A reminder that in our shared humanity,
Goodness prevails, shaping our destiny.

Mistaken identity

When I first came here, I had to get my paperwork together, so I couldn't work initially. I did odd jobs to survive, and I met a lady whom I worked for, doing things like shoveling snow and odd jobs. She also let me rent a room. That was how I managed to get by. Eventually, I got everything sorted out, and I was able to work. Since I've been in this country, I've stayed out of trouble. I've never been arrested, and I try to treat people well and avoid any kind of trouble. I don't even have a speeding ticket. Being a good citizen is very important to me.

There have been times since I've been in the United States when I found myself in strange situations. One day stands out clearly in my memory. I was preparing for an overnight shift and stopped at a Jamaican restaurant to grab something to eat. I had a craving for a beef patty, and that place had really good ones. While waiting in line to order my food, there was a guy staring at me. I didn't know why, but I'm glad I didn't panic because it ended up saving my life.

Little did I know, this guy had been shot not long ago, and he thought I resembled the person who had shot him. I had no idea about this, but he went to his car, grabbed a gun, and was preparing to shoot me. I didn't know him at all, and I wasn't the type of person who got involved in that kind of trouble. He mistook me for someone else, and I almost lost my life due to mistaken identity. He had planned to shoot me as I exited the store and headed to my car. I paid attention and sensed that something was wrong because of the way he kept staring. I took my time walking out, and because of that, he realized I wasn't the person he thought I was. He called out to me, and I hesitated, thinking maybe he needed something, like food. At that moment, I had made up my mind to cross the street and give him $5 to get something to eat, thinking he might be someone in need. But I went to him, and I was shocked and scared when he told me he was about to shoot me because he thought I was someone else. He tapped my shoulder and said, "I almost killed you." I asked, "What? What did I do? I don't know you." He said, "Don't worry about it. I thought you were somebody else, but you're much taller." He showed me the gun, and I was terrified. I had never experienced anything like that in my life.

He went on to explain that he had been shot by someone who resembled me, and he survived. He said he thought I was that person at first and was glad he paid close attention because he would have shot an innocent man. Then, his friend arrived, and he retold the story. Both his friend and I looked uncomfortable. I have to admit, I was scared. I didn't know if this man had mental health issues or what he was capable of. He said he was waiting for his curry goat when he spotted me and thought I was the person he mistook me for. I was relieved to have survived. I sent money back home and told my parents to call people over, cook food, and celebrate because I had survived something. I told them what happened. Many people lose their lives due to mistaken identities. I knew I had a purpose, and from that day on, I really tried to be myself. I always help people, but now I go above and beyond.

This incident made me realize the fragility of life and how easily it can be taken away due to misunderstandings or mistaken identities.

After that encounter, I became even more determined to make a positive impact in the world. I started to actively seek opportunities to help others and contribute to my community. I volunteered at local shelters, organized donation drives, and mentored young individuals who needed guidance. I wanted to use my own experiences to inspire and empower others to overcome challenges and make a difference in their own lives.

Additionally, I realized the importance of raising awareness about the consequences of jumping to conclusions and making assumptions about people based on appearances. I shared my story with friends, family, and even through public speaking engagements, hoping that by shedding light on the dangers of snap judgments, we could foster a more inclusive and understanding society.

As I continued my journey, I never forgot the importance of education and its power to uplift individuals and communities. I made it my mission to support educational initiatives back in my homeland, focusing on providing access to quality education and promoting literacy. Through partnerships with like minded individuals and organizations, I aspired to open a bigger school that not only taught reading and writing but also offered practical trade skills, equipping young people with the tools they need to build a better future for themselves and their communities.

I also cherished the dream that my book would serve as a catalyst for change. I hoped that by sharing my experiences, struggles, and triumphs, it would inspire others to join me in my mission, prompting people to come together and lend a helping hand. I believed that together, we could create a ripple effect of compassion and support, ultimately eradicating illiteracy and improving the lives of those in need.

Through all the challenges and obstacles I faced, one thing remained constant: my unwavering determination to make a positive impact and leave a lasting legacy. The incident that nearly cost me my life served as a turning point, igniting a fire within me to never give up on my dreams of helping others. With each passing year, I would take steady steps towards my goal, laying the foundation for the future school, gathering support, and spreading awareness about the issues I deeply cared about.

While the road ahead may be filled with hardships and setbacks, I am committed to staying true to my purpose and making a difference in the lives of those who need it the most. I know that together, we can build a brighter and more inclusive world, one where no one has to live in the shadow of mistaken identities and where education becomes a powerful force for positive change.

And so, I forge ahead, driven by the desire to bring light to the darkness and to make a lasting impact on the lives of others. This is my journey, and I am determined to see it through, no matter the challenges that lie ahead.

In life, we strive to be the best version of ourselves, avoiding negativity and embracing positivity. However, there are times when unexpected situations arise, testing our resolve. One such incident that profoundly impacted me was when I, as a law-abiding citizen, found myself facing trouble due to mistaken identity. It was a harrowing experience that I wouldn't wish upon anyone. Despite being a good person, I learned that even the best intentions cannot shield us from the unexpected. It served as a reminder to always remain vigilant and aware of our surroundings. As an immigrant, I have encountered various challenges, and through them, I've gained a deeper understanding of the neighborhoods to avoid. Through hard work and determination, I have managed to improve my living situation, moving from a troubled neighborhood to a safer one. These experiences have shaped me and highlighted the importance of resilience and perseverance in the face of adversity.

CHAPTER 11

ACTS OF KINDNESS IN THE AIRPORT

In the airport's hustle and bustle, minds solely on their destination,

People are too engrossed in their phones, lacking consideration.

A place where empathy is scarce, concern for others fades,

But amidst it all, I had encounters that left me amazed.

A few instances stood out, etched deep within my heart,

When strangers showed kindness, playing their part.

In the midst of chaos, they extended a helping hand,

Reminding me that small acts of kindness can make us grand.

Whether it was assisting with luggage or offering comforting words,

These acts of compassion resonated, like the sweetest melodies of birds.

The airport, where people rarely stop to lend a hand,

Yet there I found empathy, a hope for a better land.

A chapter inspired by these moments of care,
In a place where self-interest often fills the air.
I hope this book inspires you to see,
The value of small acts of kindness, how they can set us free.

For the memories stay with me, a lasting impression, 8.30am
In the airport's rush, these acts brought a sense of progression.
So let us pause amidst the chaos, and extend our hand,
Embrace empathy and kindness, in this busy land.

If you're early, why not let someone in a hurry take your place?
A simple act that shows compassion, a smile on their face.
These stories I share, from the depths of my soul,
Encouraging us all to make kindness our goal.

In the airport's busy swirl, let's make a change,
Bring empathy to the forefront, let compassion rearrange.
For even in the busiest of days, when time seems to fray,
Small acts of kindness can brighten someone's way.

So let us remember, in the rush and the strife,
To embrace the power of empathy, throughout this journey called life.
For amidst the airport's chaos, let kindness guide our flight,
Transforming the world with love, shining a beacon of light.

In the bustling airport, where people are solely focused on reaching their destinations, lost in their own worlds, blocking out conversations with earphones and screens, their minds consumed with personal agendas, the rush obscuring their connections. But amidst this self-absorbed atmosphere, acts of kindness break through, moments that stand out amidst the noise and haste, leaving a lasting impression.

One such moment occurred at a crowded coffee shop within the airport terminal. A weary traveler, his face worn with fatigue, approached the counter to place his order. As he reached into his pocket for his wallet, panic washed over him. He realized with a sinking feeling that he had misplaced it somewhere along his journey.

Frustration and worry consumed him as he contemplated the consequences of losing his identification and funds. Just as he was about to resign himself to his misfortune, a stranger next to him intervened. "Don't worry, my friend. I'll cover your order," he said, flashing a comforting smile.

The traveler, overwhelmed by the stranger's generosity, stammered his thanks. As he watched the stranger pay for his coffee and snack, a sense of relief washed over him. It was a small act of kindness, but in that moment, it meant the world to someone facing unexpected adversity.

Meanwhile, a few steps away, another act of kindness unfolded. A young woman, burdened with multiple bags and a restless toddler, struggled to keep up with the fast-paced flow of the crowd. Her face etched with exhaustion and frustration, she desperately tried to juggle her belongings while keeping her child from wandering off.

Observing the scene from a distance, a middle-aged man with a warm smile and gentle eyes sensed the woman's distress. Without hesitation, he approached her and offered a helping hand. "Can I assist you with your bags? It looks like you could use some help," he said, his voice filled with genuine concern.

The woman, taken aback by his kindness, gratefully accepted his offer. As he effortlessly carried her heaviest bag, he engaged the toddler in playful conversation, making the child giggle with delight. The weight of the world seemed to lift from the young mother's shoulders as she walked beside him, grateful for the unexpected support.

These instances of compassion in the airport remind us that amidst the chaos and self-absorption, there are individuals who go out of their way to make a difference. In these fleeting moments of connection, strangers become allies, and the burden of our individual journeys lightens.

The airport, often seen as a transient space where people come and go, becomes a canvas for genuine human interaction. It serves as a reminder that no matter how busy or preoccupied we may be, there is always an opportunity to extend a helping hand, to offer solace to a stranger, and to restore a sense of community in a world that sometimes feels disconnected.

As we continue our journeys, let us carry these moments of kindness with us, spreading empathy and compassion in our own spheres of influence. For it is through these small acts that we can create a ripple effect, inspiring others to be agents of kindness and weaving a tapestry of humanity that transcends the boundaries of time and place.

During the pandemic, airports had strict regulations, especially for international travel. All necessary documents, including proof of vaccination, were required. I found myself at the airport, where I encountered a man who was traveling to Sierra Leone. However, he was unable to present his documents, and the airport staff refused to assist him. Without internet access at the airport, they informed him that if he couldn't retrieve and print the necessary documents from his email, he wouldn't be allowed to travel that day. The airline agent showed no willingness to help him.

As I stood in line witnessing this scene, I felt a strong sense of empathy for the man. He appeared disheartened as the agent informed him there was nothing they could do. He seemed ready to give up, and that's when I decided to 80 approach him. Although we were strangers, I wanted to see if I could offer any assistance. He explained that he had no internet access on his phone to retrieve his vaccine documents, and without them, he wouldn't be allowed to board the plane.

I told him that although we had just met, I was willing to help him as best I could. I took out my phone, logged into the website, and entered all the necessary information for him. Finally, he was able to access the required documents, and he was allowed to board the plane. However, my own journey encountered a hiccup when I faced trouble with my luggage. I was informed that I would have to pay an additional fee due to the extra weight. This was because I always carried books, pencils, erasers, and other school supplies to donate to teachers in my home country, Guinea, which is near Sierra Leone.

It was a process that could potentially cause delays and extra expenses. However, the man I had helped earlier stepped forward to assist me, ensuring that we wouldn't miss our flight. He kindly offered to carry my bag since he didn't have any luggage himself. Thanks to his selflessness, I ended up paying nothing extra. In that moment, he returned the kindness I had shown him. Although it may seem small to others, it meant a lot to us that day. It highlighted the significance of helping one another.

We successfully boarded the plane, and to our surprise, my seat was empty. The man asked if he could switch seats to sit beside me. Throughout the long plane ride, we laughed, talked, and had a great time. It was a small act of kindness that connected us. If it weren't for him, I would have had to spend extra money on my luggage, and if it weren't for me, he would have missed his flight. That day, both of us emerged as winners due to our kind hearts and generosity.

If more people could show empathy and engage in small acts of kindness toward one another, the world would undoubtedly be a better place. Life could become easier if we simply extend a helping hand to those in need. Let us be more humane, compassionate, and considerate. By embracing such values, we can create a more harmonious and caring world.

My dad was sick, so I had to ask for an advance travel document. A form of document you can get in an emergency, but you can only visit one country, and it has an expiration date. If they give you 30 days and you go more than 30 days, then you will be denied to come back into the US, and you have to start your process all over again. You have to follow the rules, or there will be extreme consequences.

I could think of a few encounters at the airport, but the last one brought about a level of anxiety I hadn't felt in quite a while. Considering everything I was already going through, these events had me on edge like never before My dad was very sick, and I had to go back to Guinea to see him. So, when I went, I visited my dad. My dad was so happy to see me. On my way back, my return ticket was on the 8th, and my document was going to expire on the 11th. I left Guinea on the 8th and was supposed to return to the USA on the 9th. That day, when I was leaving, I was sitting in a car, and I noticed my shoe had broken, and I couldn't walk in them. The glue had made them come apart. So, I went to the shoemaker to get my shoes fixed. It was kind of a farmers market where people sell, trade, and fix things. They create jobs because there are not a lot of jobs back home.

There were a few different shoemakers, but among them, there was one who was disabled. He could not walk and had to use a stick to walk. So, when any customers came, everyone would be rushing, trying to get the sale, but he could not do that because he couldn't walk. I said to myself that I wanted to get him to work on my shoes because I'm sure that he doesn't make a lot of money since the other people run to get all the sales and he can't do that. So, I chose to have empathy for him and chose to spend my money at his business. I called him over and told him I needed him to fix my shoes. All of them started running towards me, but I told them no, I want to work with him. I gave him the shoes to fix. It cost 1000 Guinean money, which is like giving him 50 cents in American money. But I had already made up my mind that I was going to pay him 10,000 franks. When I gave him the money, he said that he couldn't take it because since he came, he hasn't been able to make any money. He couldn't really get to the customers in time, so he doesn't have any change. I said, no, you can keep the change; it was a tip. The man had a tear in his eye. He prayed for me, saying that whatever adventure I have today, God should remove any obstacles in my way. He was so happy to receive that much money as it could go a long way. I cheered him on.

I was about to fly out that day, and I had no time to waste because I had to renew my papers in the US. I missed my flight because of a big protest that was going on, blocking traffic, and I didn't make it to the airport on time. The next day, I went back to the airport so I could get another ticket. It was the 9th. I wouldn't be able to travel the next day until the 10th and be in the USA on the 11th, which is the day that my paperwork had to be renewed. If I entered later, I wouldn't be able to stay in the country, and it was now my home. I would have to go back to Guinea West Africa and start the process all over again. The only money remaining with me was 700 dollars. I went downtown to get a ticket, and they said the only ticket they had for me to travel and get there the next day was only business class, and it cost 7,000 dollars in Guinean money, and I knew I didn't have enough. I went to another plane, and they said 8,000. I went to the next one, and they said 3,500, and I only had 700. I didn't even have a phone, so I removed 100 dollars from my 700 and bought a phone so I could make a phone call. But that wasn't successful either because I had to do a lot to program everything, and it was already 4 o'clock, and they were closing the office. So, I started praying and remembered the prayer the disabled guy prayed for me. I said, "God, if I gave the man in need the money with all my heart, please help me find a way out of this trouble. If I don't get into the US by tomorrow, then my documents will expire, and I will be in trouble, losing my documents, home, job, everything."

No sooner had I finished that prayer, I saw a guy right in front of me. A person that I knew before, who used to visit us in the USA, had a family in Guinea. When I explained my problem to him, he let me borrow 4,000 dollars in Guinean money. I was able to buy my ticket just on time with the 4,000. We went and ate food, and the next day, I flew in and got there just in time. I entered just in time. Where you do good for people, God is going to make a way for you. I'm not saying that you won't have trials and tribulations, but overall, God will be there for you. 'Good Karma'

In the land of courage and trials,

Where dreams unfold and hope beguiles,

A tale of resilience and strength emerges,

As life's tempestuous storms it surges.

Born in Guinea, a land of beauty,

With siblings aplenty, love a sacred duty,

You navigated childhood's intricate dance,

Amidst war's chaos, you found a chance.

With candlelit nights and playful bickers,

You embraced joy and bonds with your siblings,

Through humble beginnings, you bloomed,

Witnessing wars and caring for the doomed.

But your spirit remained unbroken and bright,

A beacon of hope in the darkest night,

With a father's sickness, you made a choice,

To journey back home, your heart's true voice.

The advance travel document in hand,

You embarked on a journey, a distant land,

To see your ailing father's smiling face,

And cherish precious moments in that space.

Amidst broken lamps and childhood games,

You learned the art of taking rightful blames,
When your brother sought to outsmart you ,
You chose honesty, standing tall with pride.

In the markets of Guinea, a disabled man,
Who struggled to compete with the swift and grand,
You extended your hand, a gesture of grace,
Choosing empathy, leaving a lasting trace.

With broken shoes and time slipping away,
Protests blocking your path, causing dismay,
You sought a way to return to the USA,
To renew your papers and not be led astray.

In moments of despair, you uttered a prayer,
Hoping for a miracle, a path to repair,
And there, a familiar face, a friend so dear,
Extending a loan to dissolve your fear.

With borrowed funds and determination in tow,
You boarded the plane, your spirit aglow,
Returning just in time to renew your fate,
A testament to resilience, against all debate.

Through trials and tribulations, you've tread,
Yet, kindness and empathy have been your thread,
A book penned with passion, from your heart,
Seeking to touch lives, igniting a spark.

And now, as the final pages turn,
A story of triumph, lessons learned,
May your words resonate, near and far,
Inspiring souls, leaving an eternal scar.

For in your journey, we find our own,
In your struggles, seeds of strength are sown,
As your book reaches the world, far and wide,
May it illuminate hearts, a beacon, a guide.

So let the ink dry, let the tale be told,
A story of a life brave and bold,
You've achieved your goal, your purpose fulfilled,
Touching lives, your mission instilled.

With gratitude, we close this chapter's door,
Knowing your words will forever soar,
A testament to the human spirit's might,
A legacy of love, shining ever bright.

THE END

"I would consider it a tremendous accomplishment if people from all corners of the world engage with this book and find genuine value in its pages. My hope is that it reaches diverse groups, organizations, and book clubs, sparking insightful discussions and fostering positive change in people's lives. I am truly grateful to each and every reader who embraces this book, but my deepest gratitude goes to those who invest their time and effort in making a meaningful difference in the lives of others through its message."

Questions for the book clubs

1. What inspired you to write about your childhood experiences in Guinea?

2. How did growing up with seven siblings shape your perspective on family dynamics?

3. Can you share more about the challenges your father faced with his illness and how it impacted your family?

4. What motivated you to seek an advance travel document to visit Guinea in the midst of your father's illness?

5. How did your interactions with the disabled shoemaker leave a lasting impact on you?

6. Can you describe the emotions you felt when you missed your flight and realized the potential consequences of not returning to the U.S. on time?

7. How did your encounter with the person who lent you money to purchase a plane ticket reinforce your belief in the power of helping others?

8. What were some of the specific trials and tribulations you faced during your journey back to the U.S.?

9. How did your faith and prayer play a role in finding a solution to your predicament?

10. Can you elaborate on the significance of the phrase "where you do good for people, God will make a way for you" in your story?

11. How did this experience shape your perception of the concept of karma?

12. What lessons did you learn from your childhood experiences and the challenges you faced as an adult?

13. How did your upbringing in Guinea influence the person you became as an adult?

14. Can you discuss the cultural and societal differences you observed between Guinea and the U.S.?

15. Did your childhood experiences in Guinea impact your understanding of poverty and the importance of community support?

16. How did your role as a peacekeeper within your family translate into your interactions with others outside your immediate circle?

17. Can you share more about the war and its effects on your childhood and community?

18. What are some of the values and traditions from your Guinean upbringing that you still hold dear today?

19. How did your experiences with limited resources and adversity in Guinea shape your perspective on gratitude and resilience?

20. What message or takeaway do you hope readers gain from your story?

ABOUT THE AUTHOR

I am Mohamed Sanusie Traore, I entered this world on March 4, 1982, in Guinea, West Africa. Among my seven siblings, I proudly held the position of the second youngest. Growing up in a vibrant family, I was fortunate to experience amazing culture and traditions.

Currently i live in Boston Massachusetts my second home, where I am actively constructing a life that fills me with purpose and joy. It is here that I am constantly exploring the depths of my being and striving to make a positive impact on the world around me.

Throughout my journey, the media bestowed upon me the nickname "The Uber Hero" a title that resonates deeply with my core identity. What truly defines me is my unwavering love for humanity. My fundamental goal in life is to treat every individual I encounter with genuine respect, creating a space where compassion and understanding can flourish.

Driven by an insatiable curiosity and a profound sense of generosity, I am committed to extending a helping hand to those in need. I firmly believe in the transformative power of empathy and its ability to bring about meaningful change. It is my mission to inspire others to embrace kindness as a way of life, spreading ripples of positivity that reach far beyond ourselves.

In this journey, I constantly strive to challenge the boundaries of what is possible and explore the boundless potential within each of us. By embracing the beauty of diversity and celebrating our shared humanity, I believe we can create a world where compassion reigns supreme and acts of kindness become our daily currency. With passion as my compass and empathy as my guide, I am determined to leave a lasting legacy of love and understanding. I invite you to join me on this adventure, as together we can shape a brighter, more compassionate future for all.

CONTACT ME AT ;

timelyintervention10@yahoo.com.

Made in the USA
Monee, IL
23 February 2024

53491670R00056